W9-ATB-379

BATS SET I

Vampire Bats

Tamara L. Britton
ABDO Publishing Company

visit us at
www.abdopublishing.com

Published by ABDO Publishing Company, 8000 West 78th Street, Edina, Minnesota 55439. Copyright © 2011 by Abdo Consulting Group, Inc. International copyrights reserved in all countries. No part of this book may be reproduced in any form without written permission from the publisher. The Checkerboard Library™ is a trademark and logo of ABDO Publishing Company.

Printed in the United States of America, North Mankato, Minnesota.
042010
092010

 PRINTED ON RECYCLED PAPER

Cover Photo: Getty Images
Interior Photos: AP Images pp. 17, 21; Getty Images pp. 5, 9, 19; © Merlin D. Tuttle,
    Bat Conservation International, www.batcon.org pp. 13, 14; Photolibrary p. 11

Editor: Megan M. Gunderson
Art Direction & Cover Design: Neil Klinepier

Library of Congress Cataloging-in-Publication Data

Britton, Tamara L., 1963-
  Vampire bats / Tamara L. Britton.
      p. cm. -- (Bats)
  Includes index.
  ISBN 978-1-61613-394-8
  1. Vampire bats--Juvenile literature. I. Title.
  QL737.C52B75 2011
  599.4'5--dc22
                                        2010009933

Contents

Vampire Bats

There are more than 1,100 species of bats in the world. Three species in the family **Phyllostomidae** are vampire bats. They are the common vampire bat, the white-winged vampire bat, and the hairy-legged vampire bat.

Vampire bats are mammals. One-quarter of all mammals are bats! Like other mammals, bats have hair. And, mother bats give birth to live babies and feed them with milk. Yet bats can do something no other mammal can do. They can fly!

Some people are afraid of bats. It is true that vampire bats may carry disease. Yet, many bats are helpful. Insect-eating bats devour millions of insect pests. Bats that eat fruits and flowers help plants reproduce. All bats are an important part of Earth's ecosystem.

*Vampire bats are social animals. Females will feed
elderly or sick bats that can't feed themselves.*

WHERE THEY'RE FOUND

Bats live all over the world, except the polar regions and a few ocean islands. They reside on every continent except Antarctica.

You might think vampire bats live in Transylvania like the vampire Dracula does! There are indeed bats that live in that part of eastern Europe. But vampire bats do not live there.

Vampire bats are also known as **New World** leaf-nosed bats. That is because they live in North, Central, and South America.

Their range reaches from Mexico south through Central America. In South America, their range extends south to Chile, Argentina, and Uruguay. They are also found on the islands of Margarita and Trinidad.

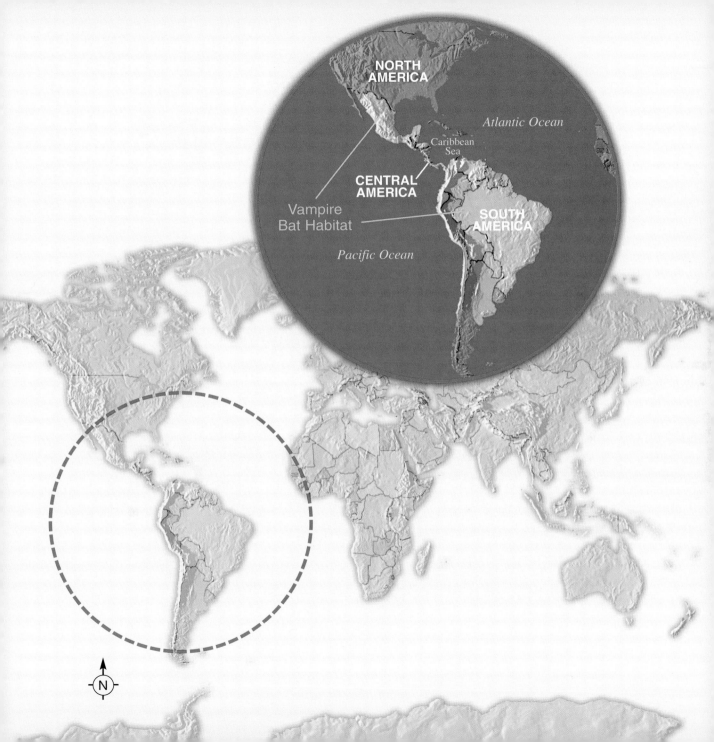

NORTH
AMERICA

Atlantic Ocean

Caribbean
Sea

CENTRAL
AMERICA

SOUTH
AMERICA

Vampire
Bat Habitat

Pacific Ocean

N

WHERE THEY LIVE

With such a wide range, vampire bats live in many different **habitats**. They live in both dry and wet areas. Vampire bats can be found in yards, **pastures**, and all types of forests. They **roost** in caves, hollow trees, old wells, mine shafts, and abandoned buildings.

Vampire bats prefer roosts that are completely dark. If **disturbed**, the bats quickly fly to a more remote part of the roost. The three species of vampire bats roost alone or in small groups. Common vampire bats may also be found roosting in colonies as large as 2,000 bats!

When **roosting**, a bat hangs upside down by its feet. Each foot has five toes. Each toe has a sharp, curved claw. To roost, a vampire bat grabs onto a surface with its claws. When the bat relaxes, a **tendon** in each foot closes the claws on the roosting site.

A colony of vampire bats roosting in a hollow tree

SIZES

Common vampire bats grow about 2.8 to 3.5 inches (7 to 9 cm) in length. They weigh 0.5 to 1.8 ounces (15 to 50 g). White-winged vampire bats also reach 3.5 inches (9 cm) long. They weigh up to 1.6 ounces (45 g). Hairy-legged vampire bats grow about 2.6 to 3.5 inches (6.5 to 9 cm) long. They weigh just under 1 ounce (28 g).

These measurements make vampire bats medium-sized bats. In comparison, a Kitti's hog-nosed bat is just 1 inch (2.5 cm) long. That's about the size of a bumblebee!

Larger bats include the fruit-eating bats, such as flying foxes. These bats can grow more than 16 inches (40 cm) long. They weigh about 2 to 3.5 pounds (1 to 1.5 kg). And, their **wingspan** can reach more than 5 feet (1.5 m)!

Like all bats, the hairy-legged vampire bat is a member of the order Chiroptera. This Greek word means "hand wing." Bats have hands that are also wings!

SHAPES

Just as bats are many different sizes, they also come in many different shapes. Vampire bats have small heads with short snouts. They have pointed ears and big eyes. But their most obvious facial feature is their pointed teeth!

The common vampire bat has dark grayish brown fur. The white-winged vampire bat's fur ranges from light brown to a dark cinnamon color. Fur that is dark brown to dark reddish brown covers the hairy-legged vampire bat.

A vampire bat has two arms. Each has a hand with four fingers and a thumb. A claw on each thumb helps the bat grab onto surfaces.

The wings are elastic **membranes** that stretch between the bat's fingers, body, and legs. The

Bat Anatomy

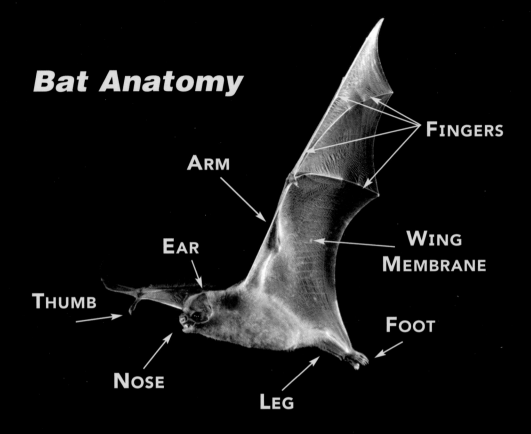

FINGERS

ARM

EAR

THUMB

WING
MEMBRANE

FOOT

NOSE

LEG

edges of the white-winged vampire bat's wings are white! The **membrane** between its second and third fingers is white, too.

Most bats have short tails. Some, like the rat-tailed bats, have long tails. But vampire bats have no tail at all!

SENSES

Vampire bats have the same senses as humans. They also have a sense called echolocation. Bats use echolocation to move around in the dark.

To echolocate, a vampire bat makes high-pitched sounds from its throat or nose. These sounds go out and bounce off trees, buildings, or other objects.

The sounds return to the bat as echoes. The echoes tell the bat the size and location of the objects. A vampire bat uses this information to fly safely, find food, and avoid danger.

The vampire bat also has heat-seeking **organs** around its nose. These heat sensors

A vampire bat can sense blood flowing just under the skin of a chicken's foot.

help the bat locate areas where blood flows just
under the surface of its prey's skin.

Sound wave sent out by bat

Echo wave received by bat

DEFENSE

Like most bats, vampire bats are **nocturnal**. They are out and about at night. So, they avoid many of the predators that hunt during the day. Spending the day in dark **roosts** also helps vampire bats stay safe. Their fur color makes it hard for predators to see them in the darkness.

However, vampire bats can still be dinner for many different predators. Bats must watch out for cats, dogs, raccoons, and skunks. Birds of prey, snakes, and large frogs will also eat bats. Large spiders feast on bats that get caught in their webs. And, some bats will eat other bats.

However, vampire bats aren't just prey for other animals. They are also dangerous predators! The

Farmers lose millions of dollars in livestock each year due to vampire bats.

wounds the bats cause on animals can become **infected**. This can lead to sickness and death. Vampire bats can also spread diseases such as **rabies** to people. Fortunately, this is rare.

FOOD

As you may have guessed, vampire bats eat blood! They usually feed on horses, cattle, turkeys, and chickens.

To feed, a vampire bat lands on or climbs onto its victim. It looks for an area without much hair. Then, the bat uses its heat-seeking **organs**. With these, it finds a place where the prey's blood flows just beneath the skin.

There, the vampire bat uses its razor-sharp teeth to cut the skin. The tiny wound is about 0.2 inches (0.5 cm) long. It is about half that measure deep. The bat licks blood from the wound. An **anticoagulant** in its **saliva** keeps the blood flowing.

The bat feeds for about 30 minutes. A vampire bat must eat about two tablespoons of blood every night. It can only go two or three nights without eating. If a vampire bat goes without eating for too long, it will die.

Grooves in the vampire bat's tongue draw blood into its mouth as it licks.

BABIES

Vampire bats mate once or twice a year. The female gives birth to one baby each time. The baby bat is called a pup. Pups are well developed at birth. They often weigh 25 percent of the mother's weight.

When a pup is born, it climbs onto its mother's chest and begins to nurse. At first, the mother takes the pup with her when she hunts for food. After the first several days, she leaves it at the **roost**.

At four months old, pups can hunt for themselves. But, they continue nursing until they are nine or ten months old. That is six months longer than most bat species care for their pups. Soon, the pups leave the roost and seek their own mates. Vampire bats can live for about nine years.

This white-winged pup was born at the New Mexico Bat Research Institute. Scientists will watch her grow to learn more about these fascinating creatures!

GLOSSARY

anticoagulant (an-tee-koh-A-gyuh-luhnt) - a substance that stops blood from clotting.

disturb - to interfere with or interrupt.

habitat - a place where a living thing is naturally found.

infect - to enter and cause disease in.

membrane - a thin, easily bent layer of animal tissue.

New World - all the continents of the western half of Earth.

nocturnal - active at night.

organ - a part of an animal or a plant composed of several kinds of tissues. An organ performs a specific function. The heart, liver, gallbladder, and intestines are organs of an animal.

pasture - land used for grazing.

Phyllostomidae (fihl-uh-STOH-mih-dee) - the scientific name for a family of New World leaf-nosed bats.

rabies - a disease that affects the nervous system of warm-blooded animals. It is passed by the bite of an animal carrying the disease and often causes death.

roost - to perch or settle down to rest. A roost is a place, such as a cave or a tree, where animals rest.

saliva - a liquid produced by the body that keeps the mouth moist.

tendon - a band of tough fibers that joins a muscle to another body part, such as a bone.

wingspan - the distance from one wing tip to the other when the wings are spread.

WEB SITES

To learn more about vampire bats, visit ABDO Publishing Company on the World Wide Web at **www.abdopublishing.com**. Web sites about vampire bats are featured on our Book Links page. These links are routinely monitored and updated to provide the most current information available.

INDEX